Guy de Charnacé

A Star of Song!

The Life of Christina Nilsson

Guy de Charnacé

A Star of Song!
The Life of Christina Nilsson

ISBN/EAN: 9783337408473

Printed in Europe, USA, Canada, Australia, Japan

Cover: Foto ©Thomas Meinert / pixelio.de

More available books at **www.hansebooks.com**

A STAR OF SONG!

THE LIFE OF

CHRISTINA NILSSON,

FROM THE FRENCH OF

GUY DE CHARNACÉ.

TRANSLATED BY J. C. M. & E. C.

NEW YORK:

PRESS OF WYNKOOP & HALLENBECK,

No. 113 Fulton Street.

1870.

TRANSLATOR'S PREFACE.

To the French author who has thus gracefully introduced our "Star of Song," we render thanks for the pleasant acquaintance first enjoyed through his efforts.

And that Mlle. Nilsson may have a place in our households, I add this, my tribute, to the earnest heart-welcome which her pure, sweet face will always win.

J. C. M.

Fifth Avenue,
NEW YORK, August, 1870.

CHRISTINA NILSSON.

I.

NEAR the southern confines of the Scandinavian penin-
sula, not far from Wexiö, among the lakes and forests of
wild Smaland, is the village of Hussaby, where dwelt an
honest peasant, who lived by his own labor. The farm,
cultivated with the assistance of his numerous family,
belonged to Count Hamilton, a descendant of the famous
Scotch house, of which this branch had been transplanted
to Sweden.

Fierce northern winds swept over the sandy soil of the
little estate, and meagre crops came as a recompense for
much toil; indeed, the very cattle seemed stunted, and the
roads were so bad that the people found great difficulty in
selling their produce.

In the midst of tall pines, glittering with hoar-frost, and
peeping out from the snows of long winters, was seen the
dark, low house of the peasant Nilsson. In those small, dim
chambers the sun-light scarcely entered, but notwithstanding
the lack of comfort evident seven children, boys and girls,
were born and brought up there, and morning and evening
little voices joined in the pious music of Luther's psalms.

Though always industrious, and with unshaken faith in God, yet the Nilsson family were sufficiently numerous to remain satisfied with the children already given, therefore neither parent desired an increase ; but when the last-born, a boy, was seven years old, the mother found herself obliged to thank God for another birth.

It was the third of August, 1843, that this eighth child came into the world, a beautiful little girl with fair hair, greenish-grey eyes, and transparent complexion—a real daughter of Odin. She received in baptism the name of Christina. At this christening came an uninvited guest as godmother—a kind fairy of the Sagas, who, leaving the child's soul to God, then and there claimed her genius.

But, notwithstanding this good fortune, in her infancy there was nothing to distinguish Christina from the rest of her sisters. Like them she was sent to a neighboring school, where she learned to read and write at public expense. The father loved music and led in the village choir, and he it was who taught this dear little late-comer the first notes of the gamut.

As she grew older, though she developed no taste for domestic affairs, she was obliged to assist in household duties, and sometimes even in the fields ; but when she was all alone in the home she would seize, as upon forbidden fruit, the bow of her brother Karl, the fiddler, and play on his violin the national airs she had heard at the village *fêtes*. One day he surprised her by admiring her skill, and indeed the neighbors were even then talking of the wonderful voice of so young a child. Karl thought so much of her talent that he felt he could double his profits if he took her with him to the fairs and weddings.

This was a happy thought, and prospered, for everywhere the pretty, popular little artist attracted crowds, charming them all successfully. Her fresh voice and frank young face; her silken hair sweeping the ground; her natural grace—all enchanted the rustic audience; and while applause resounded skillings were showered into the wooden platter which the child modestly handed around.

Was it chance, or the will of her fairy godmother, that occasioned a fortunate meeting at this time?

It was at the fair of Ljungby that this encounter occurred, when the magistrate Thornerhjelm found himself in the midst of a crowd, loudly applauding two little wandering musicians playing and singing in a corner of the field where the show was held. The magistrate paused to listen, and from the lips of the child of Smaland the simple Scandinavian melodies came as a breath of innocence. M. De Thornerhjelm was more than pleased—he was attracted to the children; so he called to him the brother and sister, questioning them of their family. The next morning the father received a letter from him, in which he offered to adopt Christina. This was not the first offer of the kind which the honest peasant had heard, for the fame of the artist-child was already wide-spread, and more than one speculator had thought of profiting by her rare talent. But the honor of the peasant and the faith of the Christian

8

always made him turn from what he considered the wiles of
Satan. This time the proposition seemed quite different,
for the family of Thornerhjelm was highly esteemed, and
there could be no doubt of their intentions. Certainly such
a protector was sent the child by Providence.

The mother was unwilling to give up her last-born, but
to her the father spoke of his strange presentiments; for
on several occasions he had dreamed of the child, and in
these visions she had always appeared brilliant, glorious, and
happy.

Was all this impossible? Did not the old chronicles
relate how simple peasant girls had become queens? And
does not the silver belt of the young maiden of Wärend,
from century to century, celebrate the deliverance of their
land by innocent hands armed with the sickle?* Had
God bestowed upon Christina that angelic voice only to call
the cattle to pasture? Had her white, delicate fingers been
formed merely to handle the shovel and the pick? Such

---

* At the beginning of the Swedish monarchy, according to the Scandinavian chronicles, and in the same province where Christina Nilsson
was born, a certain Blaenda saved the country from invasion by the
Danes. Blaenda invited the chiefs of the Danish army to a festival, at
which she assembled the prettiest and most courageous young girls
of the province, and when the men were excited by wine, each maiden
drew from under her dress a sickle with which to mow the grain, and at a
concerted signal slew her partner; Blaenda reserving for herself the chief.

In our own day, the young maidens of the province of Wärend still
wear on *fête-days* a silver girdle fastened by a clasp, on which is wrought
" the hall of the *fête* of vengeance."

reasoning was unanswerable. So the mother yielded and De Thornerhjelm's offer was accepted.

Christina soon endeared herself to her benefactor's household, and even at that period exhibited the clear mind and quick discrimination which among the peasantry replace education and knowledge of the world. Her correct behavior, general intelligence, cool and determined character, displayed while yet a child, properly foretold the firmness and prudence which her self-reliant life has more completely developed.

Mlle. Nilsson is the sole manager of all her theatrical business, conducting it so well that the most experienced could learn from her.

But we will return to the château de Thornerhjelm, where brilliant *fêtes* and continued entertaining made the time pass pleasantly. A *musicale* was given by the magistrate, at which Mlle. Valerius, a favorite singer, and afterwards Baroness de Luyhusen, expressed a great desire to hear the little peasant whom everybody praised. She was gratified, and the child sang for her, when she at once wished Christina transferred to her especial care. The Thornerhjelms agreeing, and the child consenting, Mlle. Valerius received her into her own home, and herself instructed her. She soon found that her judgment had not been at fault, for the uncultured voice possessed germs of rare talent.

Christina also evidenced great aptitude and perseverance, both of which were fine elements for future success; but the period for other instruction now arrived, for she was of

the age when young girls are prepared for communion ;
therefore, that she might be better instructed, she
was sent to a good boarding-school at Gothemberg,
where she remained two years. Afterwards she returned
to M. De Thornerhjelm, who took her to Stockholm.
There, under the direction of an able professor and composer, M. Franz Berwald, Christina again commenced to
study her favorite art with earnest zeal. In a short time
she acquired great proficiency on the piano, and from her
intimate acquaintance with the works of the German masters became a perfect musician.

A vague ambition now began to agitate the soul of the
young girl, for the name of Jenny Lind, the pride of Stockholm, and then at the height of her glory, was the theme of
every tongue. Christina could not listen to all this without
some emotion, for under a cold and calm exterior these
beauties of the north, in all ranks and of every caste, pos-
sess that indescribable fire of blood which amounts almost
to audacity. Indeed these Swedish women are endowed
with a hidden intensity, a restless daring, leading them on
to all hazards, fearless of consequences. At this time the
young girl was also haunted by her father's visions, and in
these dreams a far and luminous horizon seemed to unfold.
Now the ideal approached reality, for the sister of Mlle.
Valerius, a distinguished artist, was about to depart for
Paris, and proposed taking Christina with her. And to this
child of the forests of Hussaby a voyage to France seemed
a journey to Wonderland. The temptation was great, hesi-

tation was brief, therefore the preparations and farewells occupied little time.

She was recommended to an English family residing in Paris, and from them received a warm welcome. As her motive for leaving Sweden had been to perfect her talent, her first care was to procure a suitable master. Professor Wartel, a distinguished instructor, visited her English friends ; therefore she appealed to him for advice, and for three years carefully followed his directions. He aspired to a theatrical career for his pupil, and often spoke to her of his ambition ; but she differed from him, less from timidity than from indecision as to her true vocation.

But one evening, after her return from the Theâtre Lyrique, where she had heard Miolan Carvalho surpass herself in " La Reine Topaze," our young artist felt herself moved by a praiseworthy spirit of emulation. All doubt disappeared, and she felt her vocation announce itself. An excited, sleepless night ensued, and, resolved to follow her inclinations, she asked an interview of the director of the Theâtre Lyrique. Thanks to the kindness of M. Wartel, she had not long to wait ;—thanks, still more, to the splendid gifts and wonderful talent displayed, she at once obtained a modest engagement for three years, at the rate of 2,000 francs for the first year, 2,500 for the second, and 3,000 for the third.

The 27th of October, 1864, witnessed the first appearance of the young Swede upon the French stage and before a Parisian public. Christina was then twenty-one years old.

II

It was at this period that the "Theâtre Lyrique" appropriated to itself the repertoire of the "Italiens." Corval wished to be the first to bring out "La Traviata," because the libretto of that opera is the translation of a French comedy. This idea could not be called a happy thought, for the continued contrast of Verdi's music to the piece of Dumas-fils is sufficiently apparent in the Italian, while in the French it is positively insupportable. "La Dame aux Camellias" is taken from real life, and presents an amusing satire on frivolities essentially French; treating also of a light morality which can neither be rendered by the music nor comprehended by the genius of Verdi. Some one has very justly observed, that only the genius of Auber could have wrought such a musical arabesque on that Parisian canvas. The requisites required for a really good musician are, first, that talent which enables him to present sentiment and passion playing in full light, and again the power to portray these scenes animate with all the resources of imagination and fancy. But what is found in "La Dame aux Camellias?"—anecdotes and the ways of the jardin Mabille !

This vulgar materialism could not sustain real sentiment, therefore the composer has entirely lost sight of the text, and this explains the contentions to which allusion has just been made, and also accounts for the extreme difficulty found in the *rôle* of this modern Phryne.

She, who was more dreamy than passionate, failed to find in this conception a just expression of her own delicate and exalted nature. She was not quite at ease with her raised glass in the opening scene at the supper; she had not the spirited *abandon* so requisite for praise of the sparkling champagne; for, from her lips, a prayer came with better grace than a *brindisi.* Even the robe of the courtezan on this innocent daughter of the fields seemed out of place, just as Parisian slang would strike as discord coming from the pure lips of Christina Nilsson.

Her Scandinavian accent, at this time very apparent, also offended the Parisians; and, indeed, the assumption of this *rôle* so entirely foreign, not only to her nationality but education, seemed robbery of the inherent poetry of her nature.

For these reasons, although her *début* had been much talked of, it did not produce the expected effect. In reference to the impression she then made on me, I find the following lines in my journal: "A slender blonde, with an eye sometimes cold as steel—an actress intelligent but yet a novice, with an accent too northern for a Parisian boudoir, for whom a robe of serge would seem more appropriate than the flounces, in which she appears ill at ease. An unequal singer, with very brilliant notes in the higher scale, dull and feeble in the intermediate, while the lower notes are veiled. Such, to me, appeared Mlle. Nilsson in the *rôle* of Violetta, which will not be her last. I seem to catch a glimpse of a star which the future will more brilliantly unveil, as the clouds now obscuring it disappear."

And I was not deceived, for on the evening of the 23d of February, 1865, this Star of the North shone upon us with peerless splendor.

What better selection could have been chosen to reveal her strange characteristics, and give the public some idea of her truly religious and musical nature, than Mozart's "Zauberflöte?" Has not the great composer in this opera, considered by Beethoven the *chef d'œuvre* of his rival, interwoven with its weird music all that his heart and mind dreamed of the ideal? Do we not find in it the marvelous, supernatural, and mystic blended with the tenderest and most exalted feelings of the human soul? To this idealism, a true type of his genius—to this pious fervor, which even the sound of the church bells heightened—Mozart united in the "Magic Flute" a psychologic insight of human feeling, of love, and, above all, of that sentiment which is the essence itself of German character.

However, it was not as Parmina, the romantic creation of the musician-poet, that Christina Nilsson attempted to personate, but the tragic Queen of the Night, with her diadem of stars; the weird side of Mozart fell to the share of this daughter of Scandinavian mists.

Since September, 1792, when the blonde Aloysia Weber, radiant in the love with which she had inspired the immor-

tal author of this opera, ascended to the clouds in this very
rôle, no such harmony had ever been heard.

When the young girl appeared before us in her dark
mantle glittering with stars, the gleaming crescent on her
brow, a fierce light in her eyes, and we heard from lips
terrible in the smile of a demon, " Oui, devant toi tu vois
une rivale !" the effect was grand.

Almost a century after this sublimest creation of a wonderful genius the gods bestowed a second Aloysia, that we
of this age might realize the true conception of Mozart's
brain. Skeptical as we naturally are, at first we believed
the vision supernatural, for it was of brief duration. But
when I listened to the notes which few have ever uttered—
the trilling, bird-like treble, those daring staccati of marvelous vibration, I felt my soul penetrated with a myste-
rious sense of this entirely German creation. M. Blaze de
Bury has justly remarked of her : "As a true daughter of
the North, as sister of Jenny Lind, Christina Nilsson has
comprehended the idea of the master. If her clear, vibrating voice climbed to heaven, it was only that from those
heights she might curse as a Titaness ; for the notes came
from her mouth as serpents of fire, and she sneers like
Hecate."

Thus we behold a simple peasant girl render, with singular power, this wonderful conception of a great master ; and
soon we will see her again the most poetic heroine of Shakspeare's genius. Is not this sufficient for the glory and the
fame of one artist ?

But those who create—writers, poets, musicians, painters, and even actors—cannot stop, for constantly the soul cries out to them: "Forward! forward!" and they go on.

In 1865, Flotow, by birth German, by talent cosmopolitan, offered to the Theâtre Lyrique his popular opera of Martha; and Nilsson appeared on the 18th of December in the principal *rôle*. I was present at the first representation, but scarcely remember the effect she produced, as it was afterwards quite effaced. Only in the spinning-wheel quartette, where the notes, clear and vibrating, contrast with the rhythm of the accompaniment, monotonous as the noise of the wheel, did she receive applause. The delicious romance of "The Rose," a Scotch melody ingeniously interwoven with this music, and to which are adapted Moore's beautiful lines,

> " 'Tis the last rose of summer
> Left blooming alone,"

produced no effect from the lips of the cold Swede.

How entirely different it seemed to me, when a few days later I listened to this very air from "La Frizzolini!" This beautiful artist made of it a sweet and tender poem, and in the pathos of the song I saw all the sadness of the great singer, who, with it, bade adieu to the scene, gathering then the last leaves of her laurel crown!

III

During 1866 and 1867, three other operas served to bring Mlle. Nilsson more prominently before the public—*Don Juan*, *Sardanapole*, and *Les Bleuets*. As the theatre where she had made her *début* was closed and locked, like a hotel to let, we find her on the first lyric stage. We have seen our star realize the ideal of Mozart, and quitting this celestial sphere, in order to assume the *rôle* of a forsaken wife, she appeared to much less advantage; for, as "Elvira," Mlle. Nilsson has no opportunity of displaying her most brilliant gifts. Her high notes are not needed, and therefore she produces slight effect. Compelled to fold her wings, she follows with uncertainty the steps of her faithless husband, exhibiting none of the feeling which ought to animate her.

It is but right to say here, that the frozen nature of the Swede fails to comprehend the strength of passion or of jealousy which sways the wife of Don Juan. Elvira betrayed shows no control, but cries for revenge; never ceasing to pursue with her burning passion one whom she considers her own. Abandoning to Donna Anna the task of bringing the faithless one to judgment, she is forever faltering between her desire for revenge and her half-smothered passion. The whole situation is explained by her words:

2

" Ah! comment pourrai-je retrouver le barbare que j'ai aimé pour mon malheur, et qui a trahi sa foi! Si je le revois, et s'il n'abjure pas ses torts, je veux lui arracher le cœur."

Has not Nilsson too much calmness to comprehend such contradictions? Is it necessary for her to impose silence upon her heart and to say to it with Elvira :

" Mon cœur, calme-toi, cesse de palpiter !"

The nights of Stockholm do not endow the fiery languor which the nights of Seville give, and when you see Elvira on the balcony you feel that she will descend, conquered by the voice of her seducer. But has this " great trouble," which rises in the soul of Elvira, ever agitated the heart of Christina Nilsson? Nothing in her rendering evidences the belief. The interpretation of this *rôle* at the Lyrique recalls a very singular fact which I cannot pass in silence, since it was the occasion of a unique effect by Mlle. Nilsson.

An artist of talent, Mme. Charton-Demeur, had the *rôle* of Donna Anna, but her voice did not allow her to properly render the difficult " si bemol," as it is written in the trio of " The Masks "; and what did they do ? Nilsson supplied this passage ! Thanks to this stratagem, to this alteration of the master's idea, the famous trio was *encored* on that evening, the 8th of May, 1866. She burst forth full and clear in this talked-of *si bemol*, descending the gamut most caressingly, and again impressing her audience with the wonderful calibre of her bell-like notes. She had need of this revenge, for everything seemed to conspire against her, even the unfortunate dialogue substituted for the recitative, where her Scandinavian accent grated harshly.

If the opera of M. Joncières, brought out on the 8th of February, 1867, had taken with the public, the *rôle* of Myrrha would have counted among Nilsson's triumphs, for therein were found traits most congenial with her national characteristics.

The air *Muse de ma patrie à la lyre d'airain*, and another, *Le silence et la mort répandent leurs alarmes*, both of noble and grand character, were recited with dramatic fire and such wonderful execution of voice that I can never forget the terror and alarm produced. A few months later her appearance was totally different in " Les Bleuets " of Jules Cohen. Crowned with flowers, she charmed with her poetic appearance. The *naïveté* of the little eclogue seemed just suited to her, and all were eager to obtain one of the ears of corn which she, as the peasant girl, distributed among her companions, singing the while a graceful and original song. Indeed, the whole house craved the repetition of the charming ballad *des Orientales* :

> " Tandis que l'étoile inodore,
> Que l'été mêle aux blonds épis,
> Emaille de son bleu tapis,
> Les sillons que la moisson dore,"

that she might sing again the refrain, in which all would have joined, saying from their hearts,

> " Allez, allez, ô jeunes filles,
> Cueillir des bleuets dans les blés."

M. Cohen did not forget to compose for Estelle a waltz,

in which song a staccato, resembling the famous success in the " Magic Flute," was skillfully interwoven. It is scarcely necessary to add that in this opera Nilsson drew immense applause, and her triumph was mainly due to her finished execution.

IV.

But the fairy who watched over the young child of Smaland had other favors yet in reserve—for the director of the Académie Impériale received from Ambrose Thomas an opera which bore the title of one of the most powerful and profound dramas. I do not know what passed in the mind of M. Perrin when he beheld a work only imposed upon him by the position of the composer. But a thought of Nilsson flashed to him then; therefore he accepted it, and engaged her for Ophelia.

This was, indeed, a *coup de maître*, for, without her, Thomas never would have attained success.

The simple power of her beauty clothed this mosaic-combination with attraction, giving to it the charm which no inspiration of its author could bestow. The *rôle* of Ophelia concentrates in one scene—the scene of her insanity, produced by the cruelty and disdain of Hamlet, Shakspeare's mad prince of Denmark, the hero whom Thomas failed to grasp, for the author's incapacity is nowhere more apparent than when he makes him sing a drinking song—but this one scene, properly Ophelia's, constitutes the whole opera, and this alone has made its success.

Mozart, Beethoven, Weber, Meyerbeer, Rossini had certainly dreamed of this wonderful work; but not one of these giants dared to touch the drama of the great English poet. And so it happened that the author of three or four comic operas, none of which bear impress of originality, risked an attempt, which has been luckily made without a fall, thanks to the talent of a real artist, M. Faure, and thanks to the good fortune of an unexpected meeting.

In the flush of the ninteenth century, the Scandinavian heroine of Shakspeare suddenly stands before us in all her pale beauty,—mad,—with her fair hair falling around her, her blue eyes strange and staring, giving life to the very stones of the court of Elsinore, the royal manor of the Dane, with all its snow-clad battlements. All the travestying, all the faults of the French musician and his assistant disappear, and the illusion is complete. It is Ophelia herself before us—Ophelia arising after centuries of long slumber.

The enthusiasm was universal, immense, indescribable when she first came forth, and certainly none of this was due to the talent of the composer; indeed, I do not presume that Thomas himself assumes any credit for the waltz, only placed there to display more completely the finished skill of the singer, any more than he can appropriate the Swedish plaint introduced by her also, and which was sung a few days before by the orpheonists of Stockholm on some extraordinary occasion.

The morning after the concert, where M. Perrin had shown much kindness to the compatriots of Mlle. Nilsson, she sang to him the melody that had attracted his attention, and this addition to Ophelia's part was decided upon. Such is the history of the circumstances which created the mad scene in the *Hamlet* of M. Ambrose Thomas.

It is easy to see here what Nilsson was capable of making this part, for it was not requisite that high art should be brought to her aid. Neither was it necessary to borrow from any other actress—not even from the young Italian who charmed us with Rossi five years since; for her own nature furnished every requirement—she herself was the original. Her Ophelia presented no studied or premeditated part, for she appeared in all her natural simplicity, and therein lay her great charm. Nothing striking or artistic in her gestures, no fervid passion in her song, cold as the skies of her own land; but an *ensemble* full of attraction, and a countenance at all times charming, rendered her irresistible.

Ophelia had risen from the dead, and we append the miracle. This resurrection inspired the poem of M. Morse:

> "A sa blancheur le temps jalous n'a rien ôté ;
> Sur le front virginal d'Ophélie elle-même
> Shakspeare seulement a mis un diadème."

But the winter has flown; we have arrived at the spring-days, and while Ophelia reposes under the cold stone of her tomb Marguerite gathers the early flowers of her garden. It is the poetic season, when Germany celebrates the *fêtes* of May. Long processions of young girls clad in white and adorned with flowers, so the poets say, descend from the hills to the banks of the river singing of this festival-season.

They carry to the river offerings of herbs, and the rapid current bears away with its tributes all the ills of the year.

During one of these *fêtes* Faust follows Gretchen, who thus replies to him :

"Non, monsieur ! je ne suis demoiselle ni belle,
Et je n'ai pas besoin qu'on me donne la main !"

She knows nothing of the world, that innocent Gretchen ; therefore she is abused as a poor village girl who, without malice prepense or intention, has killed her mother, brother, and infant ; finally losing the small amount of mind and happiness which nature bestowed.

Marguerite symbolizes pure love, for she is unchanged even in the midst of her heavenly glory, remaining, as Daniel Stern so beautifully described, "the innocent and simple young girl who has sinned and suffered. She is neither stoic nor heroine, the poor child, but a sweet young Christian. She has no knowledge of anything, nor does she wish to know anything but to love. To love with all the strength of a heart in which sense has but little part— therefore has she remained pure and innocent, even in her crime." I will not examine how far Gounod, tempted by the tragedy of Gœthe, has comprehended the genius of the German poet. The work of the French composer shows, from its first to its last page, what distance separates the two minds. The grand inspiration of Gœthe soars far beyond the scope of the French artist, who, with affected mannerism, caressingly touches him with his feeble brush.

Was it possible for him to ascend to the cloud-capped heights of German poetry while his pretty little *genre* pictures could not even stand the test of the Académie Impériale ?

I wish, *en passant*, simply to prove that if Nilsson failed to render the coquetries of the composer of Faust, so faithfully interpreted by Miolan Corvalho, she, at least, comprehended the creation of Gœthe.

It is in all the simplicity of the heart that first begins to unfold itself that she says the two verses :

> " Je voudrais bien savoir quel était ce jeune homme,
> Si c'est un grand seigneur, et comment il se nomme."

Her face does not change here, nor does she express, as did her predecessor, a kind of shame, a bashfulness not in her. Gretchen does not yet know evil, and with all the *naïveté* of a sweet and innocent impression she dreams of Faust.

Perhaps if Mlle. Nilsson had sung the ballad of the " King of Thule " in a more subdued voice it would have seemed more appropriate. In the jewel scene she very properly puts aside the French affectation, decidedly out of place on the lips of a simple German girl. But in all the innocence of her soul Gretchen takes the key of the casket which she unexpectedly finds upon the threshold of her door.

> " Je ne fais, en l'ouvrant, rien du mal, je suppose !"

says the young girl, and her eyes, quite dazzled by such unknown riches, become the accomplices of Mephistopheles. True feminine coquetry, child-like vanity, the love of or-

nament innate in all women, whether princess or village
maiden, induce her to put on the jewels to adorn her
beauty. Gœthe thus understood this, and so wished it, and
the new Marguerite has done well not to conceal her secret
joy when, on looking into the fatal mirror, she realizes that
she is so beautiful. Night comes, and the two lovers sing,
with no witness save the stars :

> "O nuit d'amour !..ciel radieux !..
> O douces flammes !"

Gretchen gathers a daisy, and, in stripping the leaves, she
asks the flower if she is loved with eternal love.

> "Oui !..crois en cette fleur eclose sous tes pas !''..

Faust replies to her, and urges her to yield to his passion. And the poor child, even beneath the gaze of those
burning eyes, still finds strength to utter the prayer—

> "Partez ! oui, partez vite !
> Je tremble !..Helas!..J'ai peur !''..
> Ne brisez pas le cœur
> De Marguerite !''

And these words were sounded with thrilling effect by
Nilsson.

Marguerite has again eluded her destroyer, though her
agitated soul has already given itself to Faust ; then she
appears at the window, and with her eyes turned towards
heaven, sings :

> "Il m'aime !. quel trouble en mon cœur !..
> L'oiseau chant !..le vent murmure !..
> Toutes les voix de la nature
> Semblent me répéter en chœur :
> Il t'aime !''..

What infinite poetry has Nilsson transfused into this scene, here presenting a picture of the purest and truest love !

In the following act she is sitting at her spinning-wheel, and while awaiting her lover, who does not come, abandons herself to all her fears and sad presentiments. If the effect here is not grand, the fault lies wholly with the composer, who fails to render the emotions now distracting the heart of the young girl.

Marguerite, pursued even to the altar steps by the voice of conscience and by the anguish of the maternity awaking within her, hears now the solemn organ as it thunders forth the hymn of judgment, and then it is that Nilsson appears the veritable Marguerite of Gœthe. This is really a soul at the last extremities, tormented by remorse and appalled at the approaching punishment, sounded by the voices of the demons as they cry :

> "Marguerite,
> Sois mandite!"

Already suffering her earthly punishment, we find her in prison, and she sings without recognizing her lover who comes to deliver her. In his arms reason glimmers again ; at last she knows his voice and all misery disappears. She believes herself saved, and rests content upon the bosom of him "whom she has loved more than life, more than honor, but not more than God." Suddenly she perceives Mephistopheles on the threshhold of the prison ; she shudders, turns away, tears herself suddenly from Faust's embrace, falls backward, and gives herself up to divine justice.

" Mlle. Nilsson," writes Paul de Saint-Victor, " is sublime in this prison-trio, where love, madness, and death struggle on the bed of straw. With an enthusiasm almost supernatural, this passionate, delirious music bursts from her lips in three different keys, ascending to heaven as a three-fold inspiration. Human voice could not do more.** "

Then Marguerite calls to her aid the angelic hosts. Her voice is heard in heaven. And while Mephistopheles coldly repeats " She is judged !" voices from above reply, " She is saved !" Marguerite's soul has ascended in her song.

V

In 1867 Nilsson's fame crossed the channel, and the "Queen's Theatre" counted her among its prima-donnas. As in Paris, her *début* was in Traviata, which she had more thoroughly studied under the direction of M. Delle Sedie, Professor at the Conservatoire. The English papers tell us that her success was very great. Then she appeared in Martha, Don Juan, Magic Flute, and Faust. At this *début* the London "Musical World" repeats words attributed to Schuman : "Ein blick————und die Welt glänzt wieder frisch !" And the critic adds : "If, as the ancients say, music is the best remedy for melancholy, one might suppose that so accomplished an artist as Violetta might become her own physician and cure herself. The effect produced by this representation was decidedly in her favor, for Mlle. Nilsson was accorded rank as a singer of the first order by all who heard her then."

Notwithstanding these remarks, the English journalists declare that "she does not play *La Dame aux Camellias* as comprehended by Alexandre Dumas, and as played by Madame Doche and the Piccolomini." Nor do they hesitate to advise her "to entirely abandon such *rôles* and confine herself to a more healthy *repertoire*."

The criticisms on the other side of the channel were not more unanimous than the French press in their appreciation

of Nilsson as Marguerite ; and her admirers far outnumbered
those who were luke-warm.   We give the words of the
" Daily Telegraph " :

" Nilsson," says Clarke, " knows her own strength, and
has confidence.   She does not hesitate to appear in a *rôle*
in which we have successively seen Lucca, Patti, and
Miolan Carvalho.   She appeared in the costume made
classic by the pencil of Ary Scheffer.   Her sweet, melodious
voice perfectly rendered the aria in the jewel scene, as well
as where the innocent child recounts the death of her little
sister.   Her comprehension of Marguerite is original and
individual; for in her we find no trace of the *abandon* and
passion to which we have been accustomed in the scene of
the cathedral and prison.   The Gretchen of Nilsson appears
to us a dreamy young girl whose nature cannot conceive
any violent feeling.   This *rôle* is full of exquisite, natural
grace, and the artist preserves this characteristic from the
moment when she places her foot on the first step of the
stair-case and rests her hand on the latch of the door ;
appearing always as though she would flee away from Faust,
while he declares his passion, remaining only because she
cannot escape from the will which triumphs over her own.
She follows none of the movements nor passes adopted by
her predecessors at the moment when the spirit of evil first
obtains possession of Gretchen."

In the same year Nilsson sang at the festival in Birming-
ham, in the oratorio *Judas Maccabeus ;* creating such a

furore that she was at once engaged for the next year to sing at the Handel festival, organized by the " Crystal Palace Society."

When the June of 1868 arrived I could not resist the desire to hear the music of the great German, so I started for London.

The day after I reached this city I heard her in the *rôle* of Cherubin, in which she most perfectly satisfies. Her Majesty's Theatre had been destroyed by fire, therefore, Drury Lane temporarily replaced it; and the small compass of this building was most favorable to the *Marriage of Figaro*. In its construction and interior arrangements this theatre forcibly reminds us of the eighteenth century, and is not the favorite resort of the aristocracy, which displays its blonde beauty in the more popular Covent Garden.

Nilsson seemed especially created for the *rôle* of the page. She wears the dress, a beautiful costume of sky-blue satin, with easy grace, and appears to the life a boy of sixteen. In a word, the rendition is perfect. Even a slight *gaucherie*, natural to the ex-peasant of Sweden, seems perfectly in keeping with this daring yet bashful lover.

The first air :

Non so più cosa son, cosa faccio,

is not adapted to display her voice, and therefore, following the example of the French singers, she does not follow the movement indicated by Mozart. Mlle. Krauss has alone understood how to render the precip- itance of the dialogue of Beaumarchais and the impetuosity of Mozart's *allegro vivace*. This air is without doubt one of the truest inspirations of the musician. In this opera Nilsson's greatest success was in the famous air:

Voi chi sapete
Che cosa è amor.

The inquietude of first love can never be better rendered than by her; therefore, the *encore* here was irresistible.

A few days before my arrival she appeared as Lucia, so I had no opportunity of seeing her in Donizetti's opera. I will, however, quote here the remarks of Clarke, so that the lack of personal observation may be supplied:

" Nilsson presents so perfect a realization of the Bride of Lammermoor that a painter, in his most beautiful dream, could not desire a fairer model. The charm of her appearance was increased the moment her voice was heard. In the cavatina, *Regnava nel silenzio*, she pleased by her captivating sweetness; while her additions to the refrain, *Quando rapita in estasi*, were given with such finished skill and grace that the entire audience were wild with enthusiasm. 　*　　*　　*　　*　　*"

If Mlle. Nilsson did not bring to the contract all the passion required in the mad scene, her own personality seemed forgotten, and she entered fully into the spirit of the *rôle*. Each sentence from her lips expressed the delirium of the heroine, which voice, look, and gesture made perfect. The Cadenza, written especially for this new Lucy Ashton, by Arditi, was extremely difficult to render ; but she over-came everything, and her acting was superior to all expecta-tions.

Truly patriotic, the English showed their gratitude for the new glory which, at Paris, Christina Nilsson had thrown upon one of the creations of their immortal poet, and shouts of welcome greeted her at the Crystal Palace, where she again flattered their devotion to Handel, the great Saxon musician, to whom, on the 18th of April, 1759, England accorded royal burial at Westminster, side by side with sovereign monarchs, not far from Shakspeare, Garrick, and all the great men cherished by the United Kingdom.

This triennial *fête* to Handel is really magnificent, and, without being present, it is scarcely possible to have any idea of it. Imagine the immense building of the Crystal Palace changed into a concert hall, with an orchestra and chorus of four thousand musicians playing and singing before an audience of thirty thousand. The effect is grand. Handel, being the god of all music-loving England, the Phil-harmonic societies sing his works from generation to genera-tion. This will explain the beautiful and wonderful execu-tion met with every third year when they meet in London, under the direction of Costa, to *fête* the musician of Halle.

This enthusiasm has in no way cooled, though a century has rolled by since his death. The perfect execution of such a large orchestra, composed of societies from all parts of the kingdom, is most astonishing, more particularly as Costa only calls them for one general rehearsal. His bow alone conducts this perfectly disciplined army—but what a bow it is ! This is the most imposing spectacle it has ever been my fortune to witness.

Nilsson sang two airs from *Judas Maccabeus* with great success ; but it was the first air, full of running trills, that brought down the house in a perfect storm of applause—a well-extorted tribute, for, though only a pupil of the opera, she now proved herself capable of rendering severely classic music. The recitation was given in perfect style, and, in my estimation, she was grander to-day, because by these tests an artist either triumphs or fails.

What an exquisite chorus is that of *Acis et Galathée!* What charming freshness—what vivacity and force in the conversation between a woman and her bird—that dialogue, naïve and charming, named by Handel *Il Pensieroso!* In the graceful as well as the severe, in truth in all styles, has this Titan, this grand and gloomy Handel, triumphed—he who refused every advance of a haughty aristocracy, and chose to live in gruff solitude.

The duet given by Nilsson and Madame Dolby Sherrington pleased me equally as well as the famous tenor air and the Ode to Love. Poor musicians of the present, sad composers of "the future," I pity your distance from such a past!

Appearing in Paris as Ophelia, and singing Handel's music in English, was quite sufficient to complete Nilsson's popularity in England; and she was now such a geueral favorite that there was a universal call for her in all the principal cities in England, therefore the summer of 1869 yielded two hundred thousand francs.

When an artist creates such enthusiasm, it is well to pause and inquire into the characteristics which seem to waken the *furore*.

Mlle. Nilsson is a true aspirant of art, a conscientious and well-endowed artist—though her acquirements result from determined energy and persevering industry—these alone enabling her to arrive at a relative perfection.

Her voice is beautiful, of a singularly clear tone, recalling the notes of child-choristers. The intermediate notes could be better. Her style is often dry and devoid of charm.

I will here add a remark which cannot displease the artist—she must be seen in order to produce her full effect.

Without being perfect, her vocalization is brilliant; her trills are not very clear nor always very correct, and I must say the same of her chromatic scale. In all respects she is not faultless; yet, in the smorzati on the high notes she is indeed incomparable, and at all times unexception-able. The voice is truly national, and for this reason she has been compared to Jenny Lind. "Never," says M. Blaze de Bury, "had Jenny Lind such brilliancy of vibra-tion, though both have the same purity of voice."

But has not the voice of this pupil of Perrin somewhat changed since her first appearance? Does it not occasion-ally happen that it is slightly flat? And to what must these changes be attributed? I answer that the explanation is a reason now too general among the greater number of singers of our own time. The method of study is entirely different, for now a mere tremor passes for true vibration. They do not understand the art of breathing, and the lungs, not properly inflated, are not equal to the task imposed. Therefore the sudden interruption, or, more properly, the cutting of notes now introduced. These efforts change the most beautiful voice long before it breaks; and these are the true dangers from which we would advise Mlle. Nilsson to steer. It is only continued study and an intimate acquaintance with the great masters that enables an artist to elevate her style and properly educate her musical taste. For only from such sources must she seek inspiration, as did David, Malibran, Rubini, Labbache, Alboni, and Duprez.

Mlle. Nilsson's principal excellence lies in her ability to concentrate in some striking scene, endowing it with her own strength and thus exercising a certain magnetism upon her audience. Her success has always been greater in episodes where the interest is heightened by the beauty of the woman, by the strangeness of her appearance, than in merely the development of a complicated plot. Therefore she reigns the ideal of an Ophelia, Queen of the Night, and Cherubim.

She, herself, perfectly comprehends this, and though when she entered l'Académie Impériale she was offered the beautiful mission of reviving some of the great works of Mozart, Beethoven, Weber, Gluck, and Spontini, she waited for a contemporary to write a part especially for her.

Either her ambition did not tempt her so high, or she

mistrusted her own strength; but whatever the reason may have been, she certainly has not devoted herself to the culture of the highest art.

To appear in a kind of *tableau vivant*, and therein gain applause; to sing a waltz, and directly after to content herself with being the heroine of Gounod in a mediocre opera, have been the modest aspirations of the new star.

Is it now necessary to class Nilsson, or to assign her a place, in that pléiade of artists transmitted to us by our fathers? Would this even be possible? But to say that she is a light singer would be as unjust as to present her as dramatic; for she has neither the lively grace nor *piquant* ease necessary for the first nor the passion of soul required for the second.

A very marked character, a brilliant individuality that admits of no comparison, assimilation, or systematic classification, she must always remain. And to how many can such praise be addressed?

We live in an age when triteness puts its stamp everywhere and on everything, and to escape this is a rare good fortune.

VI.

When the little village singer, the poor child-violinist, now become the Queen of Night, was welcomed after her long absence from her old home by a chorus of young maidens of Málmö singing the national air, the pale face shone with modest pride, and the blue eyes were all dim with tears! But it was not pain that heightened the flush upon her cheek, nor did a single sorrow embitter the drops she could not hide.

It is not easy to describe the glad pride that filled the house of the Nilssons when, followed by a long procession, Christina once more crossed the threshhold. There were warm, tender embraces then, and broken words of welcome, which joy scarcely allowed utterance to; for the father's dreams were all accomplished, and the pious hearts could only thank God as their "amen" sounded.

The next day the whole family attended service at the church of Skatelö, repeating their thanks to the kind Father who had so abundantly blessed them. With wrapt attention Christina listened to the simple, earnest words of the good pastor, and when he had finished his sermon rose with the congregation. The psalm selected was the four hundred and sixtieth; at the second verse there was a hush through the church; and then a pure, sweet voice, not unfamiliar to some, sounded through the little building, thrilling each heart that had so lovingly greeted her home. And when the last note died, and the benediction was pronounced, they eagerly pressed around her, sorrowful as well as glad, for they knew that she must leave them soon. They pointed to the straw hat of the loved one, where a swallow with out-spread wings confined her floating veil. Was this an emblem ?—for a very few days after her duties called her away ! When she will return, only the fairies know. But the daughters of Sweden do not forget their home, neither does their love of country die.

The little, low house, with its coating of ochre, now belongs to the family, for the affection of the daughter has bestowed upon the father the farm he once cultivated for another. And mid the peace and competence thus provided he will pass the quiet evening of his life, watching patiently each spring for the wandering swallow that will some day return to her native sky.

www.ingramcontent.com/pod-product-compliance
Lightning Source LLC
Chambersburg PA
CBHW021448090426
42739CB00009B/1685